Dirt

Michael Lewis

Michael Terence
Publishing

First published in paperback by
Michael Terence Publishing in 2020
www.mtp.agency

ISBN 9781913653378

This book is dedicated in loving memory of
my late father John Alan Walker and
late friend Doyle Pennington
- the people who gave me life

Contents

Sunset Sea

I swam the white tiled sea
It sparkled in the blind
I lost my step ten times
Ten times or more I'd find

A green and yellow bay
No wrong or evil way
A peaceful piece of time
My eyes began to rhyme

The sky began to bleed
The moon stood up to stretch
We rolled along the ground
The best things that we found

A rotten timber frame
That couldn't spell its name
I saw us in the setting
A second's worth of letting

Blooded Collaboration

Me and mine we jilt
He and she in discipline
Her and I are unknown
She and he belong

Like water without a well
We wander without form
Like ink without a printing press
We slither never silent

Like trees concern their roots
They pair their pears paternally
Like air to all conditioned
They balance never bored

Me an' mine we flutter
He and she they dig
Her and I we glitter
She and he are selfless

Like flowers me and mine
Picked and passed then rot
Like trees he and she
Forever young but rushed

Begging Nostalgia

In every archived retina's file
Or every mannerism marked in sand
And all of what brings me youthful peace
And all of the pieces and all of the parts
Brings the silk to a blinded start

A shaded upward feeling
A racing outward thought
A tepid tap with wasteful ink
When pleasant colours I try to drink
I fail for now like an unblocked sink

The morning sun from yesteryear
Like any poison
Or any chemical
Tastes and feels like an opiate

But all of lives feel goods
And all of my angels
I try to handle
And I try to deny
But the younger I wants more and more

And the youthful me isn't satisfied
My skin through tolerance
Turns to leather
I want my early feelings

But to quench my thirst and to feel so young
I am undoubtedly fascinated
To a feeling that cannot be felt
As my universe is only mine
And yours is yours alone
Everything that I want is measured
But I wish if only one
That I couldn't tolerate the greatest feelings
As then each time they would feel as heavy

Divorced Delusions

Take me from the bottom
And marry me to belief
My heart is counting backwards
My mind is underneath

Carry me to the sky
Divorce me from delusion
My heart can't keep a beat
My mind is an illusion

Sit me in between
And court me coronation
My heart has almost stopped
My mind is in restoration

Grant me fits and starts
Engage me to contrast
My heart belongs to nothing
My mind begins to cast

Lonely Eternal Time

Sometimes I look at my watch to make sure
I'm still alive
Nothing reminds us we are dying like a
clock's face
If I'm dying
I'm still alive
And nothing reminds me I'm still alive like
the face of a clock
The face of death
Times face

Time and its ticking
Aligns us to life
Time and its ticking
Frightens us to death
Time and its ticking
Cannot die
Time and its ticking is infinite

Sometime in time
Time will be alone
Time needs me more than I need time
Time needs you more than you need time

There is a certainty in life
And I think that it is
That time cannot end
Where can it go
I cannot last forever
I can only live among nature
Among greatness
Among God
Nothing lasts forever
But time can never end
And when there isn't a being or a breath
Or a pulse or a presence
And when we forget we count
And nobody can clock it
Nobody to count
Nothingness in alignment
And alignment to nothing

Then he or she will be alone
Time will be alone
In darkness in deafness
Without music without motivation
No laughter no life
And nothing to live for
With nobody to frighten
With nobody to fuck

In its concept it cannot stop
Sometimes I look at my watch and wish it
would freeze

Sanitation

As the sun rewards the day
With pearls in perfect ways
I stand belonging to guilt
A river carries silt
And I cannot but kindle
A lust packed in a thimble
A pocket full of hate
A mirror serves a state
I can't but carry on
The best has been and gone
And as for now I'm trying
To keep the crows from crying
I can pick out precious parts
The sun picks up and starts
I'm mourning for the moon
To sanitise me soon
To saturate the sky
Evicted from my eye

I need a silent spell
To rest and then rebel
I need a hired hand
To sell me to the sand

Mystics in Me

Wisdom is wanting
Wisdom is waiting
Wisdom is willingness
To give in to yourself

Mystics in me
Marvel in melody
Mystery in you
Give yourself to me

Opulence in opposition
Oppression in ignorance
Alluded in us
I want you

The Dead Devil

Living is an ache
Living is a lake
Full of floating fish
And priced up poisoned piss

Living is a stench
Living is a trench
Rimmed with rats and rain
The dead dwell down a drain

Living is a lie
Living is a pie
Baked in blood and breast
Indulge in inverted incest

Dying is a right
Dying is a kite
Sailing skies like seas
Elegantly eased

A Collided Citrus Sight

If the day gives you the sun
You're graced to see your eyelids bleed
A collided citrus sight
An opal orange offering
Will warm your beating heart
And put your mind at rest
For this is my favourite thing in life
A flavoured freedom thieved
No more cold poverty
No more deep famine
A collided citrus sight
An opal orange offering
A flavoured freedom framed
This is my favourite thing in life

A Beautiful Broken Home

Our days were spent on corridors
A crevice away from cruelty
And quilted carpets a luxury
And a credit to live unclean

Games were named after a defeated feeling
Games were named after bullets
Games were plucked from the imagination
Games never cost a wage

And studied we were to be free
A Bachelor's honours in modesty
A degree in how to be penniless
We learnt how to be untold

Thank you brother and sisters
We've managed a marvellous spin
We were led to believe we were robbed
But it's bled out to see us all win

Colour Served

Colour is the creed of creation
Picked to profit people
Penned in plants
Flogged in fruits
Judged as jewels

A ruby red is rich and radiant
It can be a blooded bulb
Or served as strawberries

Green grass gives a smell of grace
Emitted in the eye of an emerald
Or an early burly banana

Offerings of orange opal
Or plant a purse of poppies
A citrus squeezed and sold

Lemon lacks the least discretion
Dark nights die for daffodils
Amber acts allusive

The Colour of Music

This is the colour of music
I hope and I worry you use it

This is the sound of art
I hope that it strangles your heart

First we begin with a stage
Or if you will a blank page

In order to fill it with noise
We must bring in a full set of toys

If you think of a drum banging chalk
Then the page will begin to talk

Can you bring in a flute filled with ink
Then the stage will light up in pink

Let's grab a trombone packed with paint
And drag it along by a saint

Can we shade it all in with a string
Is there anything else we can bring

This is the colour of music
I hope and I worry you use it

This is the sound of art
I hope that it strangles your heart

Classical Incense

My scene is produced
I am in blindness
An offering from a flute
And graced by the smell
Of my first memories

My scene is belonging
I can't see
The warmth from strings
And a smell of voodoo
Let's make memories

And in my blindness
Warmth
And grace
I'm inviting you to my scene
To imagine

The presence of sound
And the entry of scent
I've spread it in perfection
And layered it in perfume

My ears can feel a melody
And a scarlet glow is all I see
As it puffs up in to my nose

My only certainty
Is in time it will be silent
And the candy in my nose
Will end in time
But not before
The scarlet turns to ash

Repeated Being

The years are just repetition
Of laughs loves smiles and cries
Of every spot that never cures
Of every chemical however pure
Of every optimist and every healer
Of a knife in the back and every screamer
Of every garden and its abundance of colour
Of the morning sun and the sleepless summer
Of the winter's warmth when we lock the doors
Of the delicate drunkard that dodged the law

And the prisons we build for ourselves to feel safe
Is the cage that controls us and what's left we call
faith

Love Froth

What is it to float
Is it to thrive
I want to get lost
In the frost
I've never floated
And chemistry should never thrift
It should glow
It should pivot
At every touch
At every stance
And every glance
To exist in a heartbeat
Lose a breath of your life
You owe it to your life
To fail to care
And fool
And thrive
Energy will only ever be borrowed
And shared
As a rhythm
It should rhyme

Pay it back with pain
Your mind will be caged
Your blood enraged
To pulse
We are made of many minutes
Give one away
Give it to lust
As you cannot get it back
Or feel it replayed
It starts as it ends
In quick spurts of life
Gone and forgotten
A feeling fired
On its one way course
A feeling of force
A force of flattery
A glimpse of greatness
For a second in sin
It will end
But it breaks in your eyes
And it lives in the now
A moment of kingdom
A feel for a flow
But a mountain must crumble

And it can't be rebuilt
As for what it was
Will be what it never is
Exist in that second
For you won't get it back
I feel I'm the highest
But it begs not to last
And it won't last forever
So live in that fact

The World's End

The world has gone gin
London white
Clear and chemical
Without transparency
I have a headache

The world has gone vape
A mystical risk
Cloudy and chemical
Not even boring
I feel polluted

The world's going gluten free
We have a choice
Independent and green
We have our say
I'm under oppression

The world's cleaning up
And good we are
Private and pale

Race in a blender
I am so blessed

The world's gone girly
Before our time
Fatty and fleshy
Inspiringly alternative
As ever I'm starved

Announcing Onomatopoeia

Cult
It sparked before it came
Blunt
It started with a flame
Wilt
It polished at its peak
Quilt
A frosted feathered beak

Stars are aching in the sky
Stars are steaming smiling pies
Keep it up and never stop
Kick a ball and watch it pop

Fill
It rained before it poured
Dill
It ran and then it soared
Peel
It squirts and sounds like smiles
Feel
A coloured collared mile

Freud's Opposition

Men in dishonesty let their love eye try
To tempt their tongue to die in a lie
A structure of strength
A position of power
For a concept of safety
An idea in the hour

How many times have you dug up your sister
Twisted assisted and stolen in sin
How many times have you told her you missed her
Callous and cold on a brotherly whim

She in denial lets her bold brain design
A father in you but you don't draw the line
A structure of strength
A position of power
A concept unsafe
And unloved for an hour

Have you ever been buried inside your own
daughter
Twisted assisted and a misuse of trust
When she jumps will you say that you caught her
Viscous and vile but typically lust

Why do we think when we start off a race
That there's one extra hurdle and one extra bend
If we refer to a love lust
As plainly a friend

Words to Play

Words to please words to play
Words are gentle words can say
Words begin to paint a part
Words are chosen lines apart
Believe in song and start to sing
Paint a part your thoughts within
Pick them strike them catch them cold
Stick them spike them do as you're told
Don't waste a word as words are bold
Don't believe them all as some are miss-sold
What I would give to conquer words
I would piece my mind up into thirds
Words are true they never cheat
Words are winters written sleet
Words forgotten words that stick
Words are rotten words are sick
Words forgiven words demand
Words are penned in summer's sand

A Failed Activist

Vixen vacated from cumulus cloud
Fascists forgiven for conning a cult
Raven remanded for soiling the Sabbath
Darkness divided from north to north east
Sun started singing for south southern peace

Aided by mind washed minions and brain-dead brethren
They take us

Squeeze
Bled
We are all but juiced
All but juiced
We kept a fraction for ourselves
And juice can flow
Let's fight

Pushing Paralysis

The sound in my senses wants my soul to play
The heat in my heart asks my hands to display
The magic in me begs my mind to shine
The growth in my gut dares my guilt to resign
The sun in my spirit tries my song to be sang

In my nakedness I shook
In my shaking I was scared
In my fear I ran away
As I ran I wasn't spared

I turned and faced acceptance
My face was fixed in focus
I focussed on the truth
And as the truth evoked us
I turned in all my lies
I spoke of softer seasons
And begged to be a tree
For righteous written reasons

New Year's Grace

We can only thread what we can
The rest I'm afraid goes to chance
This year I will meet every one of you
This year I will learn how to dance
For the end is a time best forgotten
Farewell to the ones we adore
We stared into the glass
And we both hated the things that we saw
Exactly what I can't comprehend
But it really wasn't too tragic
It was nothing that rum couldn't mend
We just can't come towards acceptance
We can't learn to love our face
But we can grind it out
A star in a dull part of space
There's something that I can't quite yolk
There are things that don't equal out
But I really am just starting
Whispers that sound like a shout

Cradling Kesh

I wanted to sit down and sing
About a sweet girl called colours
To look in her eyes
And watch them get fuller
To brush past her lips
And watch them start to stutter
To watch her tense shoulders
Fall back like hot butter
I wanted to hold her when she felt she'd tried
And ask her about all the times that she'd cried
To re think a chance
When she stood up and danced
To remember a tear when it followed a smile
To catch her a star on its final bright mile
To look at her face
As I pull out an ace
And laugh at a time
When I made it all rhyme

A White Heart Drowning

Today I will wear a symbol
A fur coat black and brindle
Branded as it warns
My pocket is filled with thorns
I'll share my secret shake
To show you that I am a snake
Tonight I'll wear a pattern
A green and yellow hat on
I do not want to tell you lie's
My throat is packed with flies
Beneath the cheeky charms
There's a fuse in both of my arms
It hurts to say I should
Come clean of all of the mud
Clasp a ball and chains
And warn what's in my veins
Before I plant a seed
I'm afraid I feel the need
I apologise and I have to say
That I'll condemn myself and keep you away

Violent Apprehension

I want you all to think like me
Just for a second to see what I see
At a time when you shake somebodies hand
I need you to start a brass band
Or kiss the back of their palm
I want you to pull at their arm

I want you to think like me
And take in the things that you see
At a time when you meet somebody new
A picture of you must be true
I need you to stamp on their foot
I want you to open their gut

Can you all once more think like me
And learn from the things that you see
They must treasure the things that you have
said
You must make them feel like they have bled
You must show the good in your soul
And spike their hearts on a pole

Beauty and The Beast

I've seen you people before
You slant at the waist
And you colour your hair
I've touted you peoples black core
When I look at your spine it just doesn't seem fair

When I watch my brother is drowning
In his own sick and piss
While you stop and stare

And I've watched you weak people ask
Everything that you have
I'm afraid you don't own
I can see through you peoples dark mask
When you look at my feet it unsettles the tone

When I watch my brother is on fire
In his own tortured rage
While you wrap him in wire

I look at you people once more
My blood boils with envy
As I know that you're loved
I've watched you lock your back door
As he sleeps in the snow while you're warmly
above

When I watch my brothers skin peel
In his own leprosy
In a casket you sealed

Killing John W

We all have people we miss
But do they feel the same can it be
Can you tell me a tale and a time
When we have wondered if they are thinking of me
Take a song where it wilts at the bridge
Turn your finger towards your jaw
Keep all your thoughts in the fridge
Forget all the murders you saw
Now think of a ship at high tide
And the times you're broke on its deck
Think of a time when you lied
And the tattoos that hug around your neck

The Sun Rests Best on You

Rage and all things attached
Dictate to us to lie to ourselves
It shames us and takes off our skin
It breaks us and makes our hands spin

I have never needed a temper
And yet I belong to my blood
It boils up and steals all of my love
It coils and peels off my gloves

And what does it leave when it's gone
It shows all my glory to none
I owe it my life as it thieves
The noise of my heart as it breathes

But I love to look at your smile
And the sun rests best on you
Your mind is the width of the Nile
And I want you to glow in the dark
I want it to rain but I don't want a cloud
As I tell tales of you folks say I look proud

Run

Breathless and Naked

I am jilted by the juice of life
I'm poisoned by the paste of perseverance
I made my bed
And now it calls me
It screams my name
It cannot be dodged
It cannot be ignored
It waits for me
It is considered a comfort
It doesn't consider
I've spent my life running
I'm a great runner
But the hell that I belong to
Is heavy
It cracks my calves
It splints my shins
My throbbing thighs are tired
My ego is exhausted
With every day that dwells
My speed is saturated
By the drags of the day

I’m slowing down
And my fate is speeding up
My bed bellows my name
And the raging rats are racing
I can run a little more
But I can never turn and fight
The fight is never fair
I’m breathless and naked

When they catch me nobody will care
Or at least I wish they wouldn’t
As the only ones that will
Will be heartbroken
As they were the last time
And the time before
And of course the first time
I can’t live with that

Meeting Judgement

I am terrified of when you will come
But I know that it is indefinite
I think I will be flat
Relaxed
Still
Awake in spirit
But senses closed
In paralysis
You elevated over me
My mirror
You will not be overjoyed with my
character
For I have failed you many times
Whilst you never left my side
Sorry will not be enough
Sorry will be my final failing

I believe you will come in my final
moments
And deal me my due course
I believe that I must climb a hill
And wrap myself in mountains
There will be my final fight
My beloved bastard breath
Will wince at what awaits

Lavished by lightning
Thorns of thunder
Bashed by bolts
Thrashed by a thousand threads

Vengeance Is Fated

I am the channel
I am the medium
I am the body

I want to take the bad
The evil
And the wrong

And fix it
Pollination
To be good
To be angelic
And right

Crack my tongue
Lick my whip

I am the light
I am the vessel
I am the breath

I want to take the flame
The fire
And the spark

And double it
Combustion

To blaze
To thrive
And to burn

Strike my gas
Spray my flint

I am the crest
I am the transformer
I am the field

I want to take the heat
The idea
And the feeling

And quill it
Dilution

To flow
To fade
And to let go

Crack my tongue
Lick my whip

Hate is deaf
Death is dead
Energy remains

Love is blind
Sight is sickly
Choice is a concept

To Try or Not To Try

If I can reach
A poet
A piper
A pauper
Or a priest

Then nature within her promise
Must let me lend
My wrist
My fist
My kiss
And my mist

And in return if they agree
Then I must thieve
Some fiction
Some flavour
Some fame
And something fatuous

And if nothing is honest
And it really exists
Then I'm going
Going
Gone
And done

I'm done
I'm dumb
I'm deaf
I'm beat

I'm finished
I'm banished
I'm mute

But still
I may
I maybe
I might

Spilt Salt

I want to talk about my tears
Then you can tell of yours
Spill your tears on me
Tears spilt
Tears told

You can cry over spilt salt
You just need me to pull

I want to buy your tears
They're in such high demand
Sold in trusts currency
Tears bought
Tears sold

You can cry over spilt salt
You just need me to pull

Tears shared
Tears drawn
Tears pushed
Tears poured

Tears spilt
Wilt
And lilt
Tears made of lilt

Tears built
Jilt
And quilt
Tears form a quilt

Tears bribed
Tears robbed

Thanks for your cries
And you can thank me with smiles

Worthless Worker

We are made of many minutes
We are giving too many away
Time that belongs to us
Is pillaged and traded with pain
Eyes have been bleeding too long
And tears each day start to spill

Why do you let yourselves lose
Have you ever lived up to your worth
Why do you offer your life
When your price is sold in screams
There is something you all must know
And think of your bubbling eyes
That nothing is how you are priced
And zero is what we are worth

And if work for today is too much
Then don't tell you feel unwell
Tell them you cannot walk
Tell them they cut off your calves
Show them you cannot stand up
Show them the weakness they want

And never be guided by guilt
As you don't owe a part of yourself
And don't be persuaded by pressure
As it's you that belongs to you
Hearts are beginning to bleed
And wrists are asking to spill

Anchor Road

Silent rooms full of colour
Peaceful air and violent vibes
But controlled
Art in every corner
Every crevice and every stage
Wild flowers attack the walls
Though they are but dead
They never lived
They bring me to life
Faces of loved ones
Some here some passed
Creations
And in itself a creation
Worldly gifts ask to be looked at
I'm taken by this shack
I want it to swallow me
I want to erupt in her gut
I want to bring it to life

And in return if asked
She might make me flame
An echo
A quaint offering
A place to call mine
A morbid reason for being here
As all of its offerings have blown me away
A modest man
A prince
I'm home

Leo Lies in London

How many more must I lose to London
My sister
My love
And now my pearls

Pearls a singer
So sing
And dance
And roar

Like a lion

Gentle Garden

I think the true gentleman and the man
that works hard to be gentle should be
sieved through the filter of a woman

Whatever is left in the flask
Or swilled on to the pavement
Whichever way you see it

Coiled in cask
Or spat on to the soil
Whichever floats your boat

Is the unfortunate soul
The beautiful soul
The lonely soul
The gentle soul
The bobbing soul at sea

The Dead Town

The world is lost in prostitution
And baked again in drugs
I'll do my best
But first I must sleep

Medusa

Lips that freeze your heart
Tongue that ties you told
Death served as a tart
The day I must be bold
Will I meet my maker
Sailing a ship at sea
Are you the under taker
Have you come to bury me
Flesh falls at your feet
Are you conscious of your card
As everybody you meet
Sinks or sank or scarred
I'll gamble on the road
A trip with my most treasured
Am I fated to explode
Is my coffin waxed and measured
Are you a deadly drug
Black widow webbing me
For I am just a bug

But a bug that's cursed maybe
Do you deal you in death
Will you deal me to the dead
And is my final breath
Dealt to you beyond my bed

My Unreachable Love

Like lights like lamps like tunnel ends
They shone
And modestly presented me
Well things don't always present
Like a lighthouse in a storm
They blared
Like a mirror in a trance
They shook
Like bright tunnel ends in busyness
At mercy from deadly speed
They blighted
Like lamps like lights like tunnel ends
Her eyes lit up in white
Like lamps like lights now corridors
An angelic horse and carriage

Clare

The birds the bees and the barking dogs
The birds and the bees
I hope she flies away

The birds the bread and the barking brains
A seeded one at that
I hope she's baked in peace

The birds the breath and both that bark
Whistling breath
It's easy if you blow

The birds the curds and the buns in icing
Lemons cut to rot
And a planted part of Eden

The gin my kin and the sin bin
That will never need to empty
For it smells like she's alive

The sun the fun and the gun that never speaks
Then help me God
As my life belongs to her

War Torn

With dirt that is finally dry
Dry for now
I've stuck to slumber for many years
And many more are posted
But now I want to live
I'm turning towards tension
And tensed by what could bliss
I'm switched on
Turning all that is bleak into something new
I hope it's good
It's been a long time
I'm turned on
Stretched from shoulder to shoulder
And paid what's owed to me
Now to dig
And try to dodge the dirt

Gazzle

And the seagulls never sang that dawn
For they had flown back to the tip
The sea had stood still but he
He had carried back
Back to the bones of his Mother's arms
But he left his love with a promise
That if such a scene should swallow him
Then a jab for all its teeth
But not in the gum
And not in the face
But snarling teeth that chew

HTS

The kids are dying
And dead they'll only be
The kids never lived
Warped in
And short of adulthood

What of my town
And the grateful dead
The dead that never made it
The grateful numb
Christ you couldn't imagine
Then say something

The fast man
The quick man
The invisible man

Well what of the man that bleeds
The man that never breathes
The one that blows
And never sighs
The empty men
The dead before born men
The dead men
Are you content
Have you begun
Where will it end
In a book

Will it be taught
It couldn't be taught as we had the best
Burn my town
And spill the seeds that it shamed
The bobbed haircuts that it blamed
The blame it cast
The blame it lacked

I'm due to spy my town
But I beg if any
That I don't visit by suit
And I don't visit by pipe

But die by swing
And swing to death
And slide to numbness
And spin to the dead man

God love my town

D'Arcy

A list of looks

The first time was ominous. A prize that picked all
eyes within a tap that screamed outsider

The second time was a new gaze. I stood merciless

When I pulled my paw to push my jaw to fix my
focus on something dull
Something dull for safety
You told me you taught. So I kissed your crown and
ran

The third time never existed. You stood,
silhouetted. And blind I was. Fixed in dullness,
dullness means safety. For me it's a woolly hat

And forth
And fifth
And sixth
And more
All sit seasoned and sizzle as my soft side pours

But most of all the second
When I dragged my eyes to a place less vulnerable

Longing Wishes

Things had changed
And things had happened to me that I
never thought would happen again
I swore I'd never melt
But my lungs had been beat
And my heart began to mush

A pale wisp had begun to blossom at the
depth of my imagination
And this time I had a chance
Slim to none but I'm surrendered
So the blade that cuts is cued
And the sharp that slices is set

But still at mercies edge
And hoping to hang even further
I'll drive my heart into danger
And I'll burn out my lungs if I must
For a chance to dance in heaven
With a gamble to let my heart rust

The Price of Trauma

I like the peace among chaos
That's why I choose it
I love to be that lonely eye
Because nothing has spun it otherwise
I'm the third in line for a spell spent dark
And the fifth of a quarter that screams for isolation
My being me is bled from a heart
I'm tranced at a pivot by you being kind
So be cold
But look sharp
And keep my being delicate
At the trough of a boil
Where once was a word spoken in friendship
Please chop it up in to feathered forks
And slice the unknown into two parts of wisdom
Then collar the part where I'm still and I like it that way
And the other that begs to be loved
By a flight in forgiveness that binds where it wilts
And the part that piles on the price of trauma

Then spill at the spine where it snaps with
seduction
And finally tell me the place where you learn
To be parted by petulance
And grace me belonging to a handful of hands
But freedom once doted
And favour once plucked
Can both stand apart as I beg from my soul
For peace in its element with nothing else framed

My Last Loss

I thought of you last night
I thought of all the great things we could be
Dreamt a little
But it was midnight

I asked myself if I should ask
I asked myself if painting minds were real
I dreamt a little
But it was midnight

I'm feeling full
I'm feeling flaky
I'm lost
It's midnight

Shall I pursue in blind wilderness
Shall I shake
Shall I stalk
It's late

Still at midnight
Still at dawn
Still it's late
Still hopeless

The Beasts and The Prey

The beasts and the prey
The beasts have horns
The prey has flesh
The cunning and the quick
The beasts have claws
The prey has pace

Beasts and prey
Which is which
One wants to hurt
One wears a skirt

Horns and flesh
Which is worse
One comes from instinct
One can't blink

Claws and pace
Choose
From sexism unjust
From power as a must

God Begin

Where do I begin with words
Have I failed
And where have I once flattered
Hazel hair and starlit eyes
Then in which I must believe
In God a creator or nothing at all
To spark wild eyes or crest wild hair
And if nothing as an infinite
Then believe me as I may
I believe in a referee
For all that's good and bad
A righteous one that blows
For good
For bad
For fair
Please send the good to going
Please send the bad belonging
I believe in a referee
I believe in hazel hair
I believe in star lit eyes
I believe in a common good

And the bad bewildered spawn
There's a dead man in us all
There's a dead girl cannot call
If not a God then a referee
A golden hazel hair
A starlit eye with nothing less
Than a whisper in my soul

Through Fields

Then the joints of my bones dissolved
It had begun
No point being alone unresolved
So I ran
There is only so much time left to think
I had forgotten
And a lonely rhyme starts to link
Wrapped in cotton
And in my mind a thousand thoughts
And in my thoughts a thousand prayers
A rhyme that runs but never sprints
A rhyme that wraps but always splints
The crest of the sky will always be red
It was bleeding
And the best of a lie will always be said
It's in its needing
The point most sharp will always unfold
It's a truth
And the joint of a harp is where its melody is told
It's in its youth

And in my mind a thousand thoughts
And in my thoughts a thousand prayers
A rhyme that runs but never sprints
A rhyme that wraps but always splints

Deathly Dreams

I’ve already died one hundred times
In dreams and in nightmares
I have lived laughed and loved
In dreams and in nightmares
I saved you once or twice
I’ve lost you more or less
In dreams and in nightmares
In dreams I’ve rolled the diced
In ghastly mares a thousand mice
If I’ve fallen asleep one hundred times
Then it feels like I’ve woken only ninety nine
So is a part of my life played out in
unconscious
And is part of unknown played out in my sleep
I’ve put out fires
I’ve rolled tyres
I’ve fled through fields
I’ve speared through shields
I’ve poached deer
I’ve coached piers
I’ve been violent

I’ve already died one hundred times
In dreams and in nightmares
I’ve lived
Laughed
And loved

Forget the Farewell

With ears pricked and yolks plucked
By melody harmony rhythm and rhyme
And all of its volume and all in applaud
Then starts the tale of a folk song that ended prematurely
So there's days been and gone where my eyes have smiled
Now nights here and now where my red blood is riled
And a time in the future before it forgets
Of wisp in commitment and all its regrets
If a pebble is tossed in to the deepest pond
Then a ripple will climb to the very shallow
If a stone is stepped on it may start to roll
Then crushed into parts and an eye for what's hollow
By now in abundance there's a gap in loyalty
And replaced with disregard

Slander never
Freedom however
A gap in loyalty
Spoilt like royalty
Smiles with flattery
Correction without conviction
Farewell

Flow of Feathers

With all of which shines and all that is dull
And what then defines and what's barely full

Then ease in design
And tease if you please
Illusion resigned
Alluded in presence
Please be here now

With all of which floats and all that will sink
And what then promotes your aged cells to think

Then fix your position
Be brisk without risk
Reduced ambition
Renounced of fear
Please be here forever

Praying for Purpose

Forever is closer than one might think
Forever is further for eyes to link
Beginning is the breadth of the first novice mile
Beginning is the length and the width of the Nile
The middle is the part that can speak for itself
The middle is the now in sickness or in health
The hurdles while prevalent should be left in the past
The hurdles since conquered are not built to last
The sign whilst you're here is a symbol unsaved
The sign when you're gone is a memory engraved
The parts that are dark should be considered short
The parts where they peak should be held in your thoughts
And all in a sum can I ask one thing more
That I never stand still as life is to be explored

Smothered in Shame

In a dim lit dwelling
With wood for comfort
And your ears are swelling
From the fuzz for noise
My nose is bubbling
My throat is thick
And it's full of fat
My shin shimmers
From standing so still
My heel aches
From standing in sick
My knees are pricked
Paggered from a push
But still they can circle
I'm making them spin
My chest is tense
And quick up and down
It's thrilling to be here in the now

My strings are springing
Shimmering like good times
And the sound
While it lasts
Will make me proud

Before smothering me in shame
But the pride in its time
Outweighs the shame in its length
So I choose to share
And to brown
To green
To spring
Shimmer
Shine
And shiver
To spend myself here
With you and yours
Live in a minute
Just the odd one
Laugh at the past as you should
And worry for your pantry
But steal the strange moment
And hold it for as long as you will

Ugly Truth

I've never been one for secrets
But I want the truth to fall softly
I want to know it all
But the truth must sparkle at worst
And then in truth I find it hard
When its beauty is so real
To believe in great things that are put to me
So maybe I want lies
I only believe the ugly truths
That shows me at my worst
The ones that put me against a wall
They're the ones I follow
So maybe if you want to show me
To hold a mirror to the good in me
Then truthfully the best that you can do
Is lie and stab my heart

Unrelated

I want to fly to greatness
But I'm stuck here all alone
Was I born too late
As I don't feel related
There's parts of me that wants to hold
hands and sing
And that makes me feel poor
Not numb
Just poor
That's the part of me that feels beneath
But there's nobody left who agrees
As I really am unrelated
I have a small number of conversations left
For now the ones left are fuelled in
chemicals
And these at times I can follow
But with this at best
And this at worst

A chemical screams for the high point
And a chemical screams for more
So right now and always unjust
I really am unrelated

Drunken Fathers Day Ramblings

I was tingly
I felt no shame
I was awake
I couldn't remember my name
I stood
I stood in solitude
I stood alone
I was paused in absence
With rage and regret
I prayed for no neighbour
And granted with this
But still
Still maybe
Still whenever
Still might
I'm ready
Ready to start
Not ready to finish
I'm vulnerable
Vulnerability multiplies
When it comes it comes

When it's gone it's gone
And the dead
As for the dead
The dead must bury their own
Bury the dead
Be peaceful
Please be at peace
Pray for peace

Early

Measure of Tenacity

Perseverance is production without reward
It's the measure of tenacity
And it's like the result of agony and sweat
Everything in the middle is joy
And all in between is freedom
I'm unlikely to rise
I'm unlikely to float
But joy
But freedom
Clasp me towards perseverance
And to keep on trying
With a tepid tapping
And rapid rhythm
Then echo

Who knows

A Gentle Whisk

All I urge for is a gentle whisk
For today I fear
Is yesterday's twin
And tomorrow's cousin
Block out life
And when it's over give me it back
Cut me
Bring me back
Today is too tranquil
Pains me to persevere
Forget faith
Just for today
Then love what you love
And beg for a break

Feral Friend

I met a man that matters
A man to save the earth
Realism and pessimism
Will cut his throat
And what he knows will erode into dust
He had a trick in his cuff
A note he used to bluff
He undermined his specialty
As those who recover do
Not me
I cool my head with discipline
But minds can multiply
I exist in different thought patterns
I'm different in my thoughts
I can fool your forensics
I can carry on in coherence
But my good man
Can he do the same
Will he wear a militant colour
Will he colour without capture
Will he deal his thoughts to the future

Will the future fail his thoughts
And will he work with me
Will he stand in judgements eye
Will he lax his fear
Will he lease his brain to me
We can try and not be hopeless
We can try to carry a cross
For he is in denial
Denial of his dear duty
As for me I'm scared of sorcery
I'm scared that I'm alone
I met a mathematician
I met a crippled caster
Will we meet in minds
Will we deal the dead to description
Can we start to catch a following
And multiply its chaos

Choking Gasping Bleeding Bled

What would you say if I told you that death is lulled in love
Have you ever died in an army of arms
Loved ones arms
Have you heard
But what if I told you that that army of arms
Were a handful of hands
Arms tensed
Hands clenched
Around your throat
And your heart
Choking
Gasping
Bleeding
Bled
Arms tensed
Hands clenched
Death is dealt by the devoted
Lust lies last
With a list that longs for life

That's my life
My mystery
My life
First you want to share it with me
Then you believe you can better it
You can make me better
But a better me is not me
Now I'm obligated to be us
I no more
We are we
And we through temptation
Become you
Are you anywhere near content
I died for you

Deal Me Dead

What of all of my criticisms
You won't be the first
Love me
Hate me
I'm thorough and straight to the point
You know where you stand
Love me
Please love me
All of my failings are at the forefront
They stare at us both
Hate me
My shortcomings are amongst us
And short they fall
Then hate me
Despise me
Call me a hypocrite
Call me a whore
Call me worse
Hate me
And in one fallen word send me to death
And deal me dead

Death can’t be worse than breathing at times
In times breathing is hard
Breathing is dull
Breathing is a push
Breath lasts far too long
Hate me

Steals Me A Sunset

When and where can I quench my thirst
What is a well and why doesn't it dry
That's my love
My love is a well my loves never dry
She walks in wonder
She moves in marvel
She speaks in sultry
That's my love
My love is a well my loves never dry

When and where can I spill my love
What is a snowflake and why is it warm
That's my love
My love is a snowflake my love warms my world
She smiles with seduction
She loves with loudness
She cries with chaos
That's my love
My love is a snowflake my love warms my world

When and where will you hold my hand
What is an ember and why is it bright
That's my love
My love is an ember my love burns in brightness
She gives me her greatness
She brings me her best
She steal me a sunset
That's my love
My love is an ember my love burns in brightness

Llandudno

Getting off the tracks in fog I felt I'd made a wrong move
What will be will be
I briskly dragged my axe and spelt my way to my digs
I never really stuck around I just used it as a head rest
The sun began to scream
Things were looking forward
And thirsty me as ever
And starving always starting
I took to my best hobby
Drinking eating and drinking more
Sleeping in folk bars
Climbing hills and sleeping more
Peddling by the sea and shore more than twice maybe
I took to maybe staying here
For forever or death or whichever is dealt first

I met a mystic that told me a tale
And wrote it before it was written
I met a broken soul that sang
And twenty years to tell
I promised to squeeze another night
And struck my axe with strings
In all my time this town has never left me
It speaks to me each day
The very least a man can do
Is to listen when the sun speaks his name

Painting Patterns

A strain of faith
A grain of freedom
A stain of greed
A pain of guilt
A height of peace
A flight of pity
A sight of hope
A fright of help
A try of charm
A high of character
A sign of trust
A lie of task

Will you lie with me here
I'm alone on my own and there is nobody near
Will you paint patterns on my chest
I'm wishing a world that would be joyfully blessed
I'm taking to talking to you as a mix
Of feelings and thoughts and a thirst for a fix

Desperate for Destruction

Dreaded in desperation
Desperate for destruction
Coiled in consciousness
Numbness never
Cradled with kindness
Tricked by truth
Ceased by seduction
Cruelty kills
Boarded by boredom
Willed to wait
Framed and forgotten
Drenched in despair
Trapped in task
Provoked by production
Armed with aggression
Picked by peasants
Reluctant to race
Forever in failure
Hyped in hypocrisy
Bitter and broken

Life in Length

You've definitely heard it be said once before
That a cell or a box is a present called day
You wake you work
You work you tire
You sleep your day
Then the day brings yet another trick
The cell or the box will flip in repetition
You wake you take orders
You take orders you're flat
You rest you repeat
Night is where I wish to spend my life
Night is quiet night is lonely
You spring you eat
You eat you love
You sleep then day

Love That's Spat and Love In Spits

First of all I would like to say never
Never would I or never have I
Lived without you or lived alone
I struggle with colour
I struggle with vibration
But most I struggle in clouds of love
And clouds above seem to spell the rain
And loud less doves pair in woven dew
This is where I start with you
And this is where I end in bruises
A love
A life sentence
And a hat that doesn't fit
Love that's spat and lust in spits
Crushed in rage endearing wrists
A belonging
A being
A shoe that fits twice
Love that sucks and lust that slices
Setting cement still your jugular spices

With all that's forgotten and all in debt
With all that's rotten and all we protect
With all that's going and all overseas
With all that's showing and all out on lease
With all this in mind as the sun winks at night
Then the day is aligned and the moon joins
the fight

Drugged and Dazed Delayed

When does pressure become cruelty
When does forgiveness become stupidity
When does noise become deafening
When does flattery become forced
Weather spells the day
Pleasure play and pray
Returning my ambition
Drugged and dazed delayed
When does trust turn to smoke
When does fear turn to heat
When does rage turn to guilt
When do eyes fail to blink
Weather spells the day
Pleasure play and pray
Returning my ambition
Drugged and dazed delayed

Raging Beauty

Because she looks so beautiful when she's angry
She looks so beautiful when she boils
Knowing what I know with time
I dread to think what I dared to do
If I'd never met her then what would be my
weakness
And once or twice when I think what if
A common thought with the least control
I sometimes smile at the deck I'm dealt

Because she looks so beautiful when she's angry
And looks so beautiful when she boils
Every lesson hot and cold
Every season drips of gold
If there never was another then who would roll my
dice
With rolling rhymes she starts to stare
A feral fuse then snaps in half
She shreds a peaceful calming time and mine
But she looks so beautiful when she's angry
And she looks so beautiful when she boils

Crossroad

If in life I had the choice between strength
and courage
Then in life alone I'd pick courage
For strength I've been spoiled
And bravery rare
Strength to endure
Courage to explore
Then the answer is there when you ask
yourself
Is life to be endured or to be explored

Passive Smoke

Wasn't it so much more nourishing when we had to sit in silence
And listened to a better diet
A channel for bias
A channel for nonsense
One for fun
And another for bias
In groups we listened
If we spoke up we were shushed
Back then that was a verbal cane
Believe me
Better schooled back then we were too
As maybe strictness of vision
And hard values of sound
Was a great way to learn
And shouldn't stay in the past
As ever I
As I write I
Cannot tell of a tale
Or lease out a lesson
Without I

Speaking of me
Then I say this
That if I could read I'd be great
But maybe I being me
Should just learn how to listen

Lyndsay

My perfect poppet springs in substance and cares with crests of selflessness
Then in time she gives too much and breaks in bursts of red
Each and every time and why I'll tell of why she hurts
As she gives the world but receives the moon and we wonder why she's blue

But my favourite part about my love is she saves the best for me
Not a circus
Not a stage
She saves the best for me

Life's Pair

I squeezed a gem and it never split
I finally tamed a tiger
I finally fed a fox
With whistles and worms I coaxed a dove and now
I'm paired for life

I picked a thistle and it never pierced
And now I'm in a daze
And now I'm getting started
With whistles and worms I coaxed a dove and now
I'm paired for life

Lennon Jamie Lewis

My boy

My boy in sum will be breath and time
And all in congestion I must let him speak
Speak with his tongue
Speak with his hands
Speak with his heart
Speak with his brain
And lastly his soul

I won't be forgiven for my part in his life
I can't be forgiven if I don't sway him great
Weak
Poor
Miserable
Wasteful in ways
Destructive

Perhaps

He must be great
He will be great

Ideas so far can come from thrust
But in time when he ages they'll bounce from
his mind and ricochet in multiplication

Then finish in genius

My boy

Going Dark

Life has given me a great one
A kind
Gentle
Fast
And fun one
Life has taken its time and time has
blessed me by numbers
Spoilt me
Loved me
Taught me
Never tricked me
Life in length has built me
Gripped me
Gripping
Grip

My Greatest Gamble

A plot against my future
And convinced my freedom thieved
Whipped and breathless for hours and hours
And petals snagged from flowers
When she calls she wants it shallow
With breadth
But without depth
When she comes she's such a creep
I'm fond of all things deep

Sentenced to a life without consent
And a pillaged part in its craft
Cradled and winded forever and ever
Like a spike that stems from a heather
When she calls she wants it shallow
With breadth
But without depth
When she comes she's such a creep
I'm fond of all things deep

Glittery Infinity

I'm a child of the planet
I see the stars before they burn
I'm as wild as the comet
From the suns scars I begin to learn
In childishness
In wildness
In wilderness
I begin to burn
I spark
I twinkle
I bubble
Flame
And think
I pour out a drink
Then I am immersed
I fall back into deepness
Depth of a rotten cloth
Now is the time to stand

Face first
Head on
Head strong
And long led
To stand and then immerse
In glittery infinity

Autumn

Woven weaving leaves leave like squeezes of love in
lustrous lullaby
A burning breath steams in wisps of shivered
struck softness
A lark at height in elegance begins to show its
wings in hidden headed breeze
And graze in infinite pause
And pick a climbing push
To paint in perfect ways

A Muse Like Fallacy

I've discovered a deathly silence inside myself
and I can't make it speak
In company or solitude I'm alone as ever
I may as well leave myself to my breath alone
To steam in seclusion
To mist in isolation
A muse like fallacy
In fortunate frames I've stood in company
But now is no time to gloat
Now is a time to divide
Now is a time like any
A time to drive alone
To row my boat alone
To swim then sink
Alone

Silent Hearts Are Wasted

A heart will always have its own identity
And none are ever mirrored
A heart in effect will boil your voice
And sink you as it drowns
But to wear it on your sleeve
Is to rope it around your neck
And to let it speak your mind
Is the most alluring act
In times your heart will double
And backed in firm alliance
But each and every time believe
It bubbles in time alone
So for me it's best to say
That silent hearts are a waste
And a tasteless heart is trapped
But a beating heart should be bold and brave
And thud in thunders of noise
Even if it's beating breath
Bubbles in time on its lonely own

The Sound of Your Eyes

Forty days from forty skies
I've never asked or wondered why
If only for one thought
I'd look for you and your eyes

And I want the night to bleed
When it's you alone I need
And I look
I look for both of your eyes

Heaven schemes and floats in love
A dead love rises up above
And if ever I'm called up
I've got to tell them you're my home

And if the night won't leave
I'll strap up my long sleeve
In warmth without the warning
The sun is out of the scoring
I want the night to bleed
Still it's you alone I need

And should you ever want some more
Then I'll drag until I am sore
I'm the one that cannot stop
You're the one that won't stand still

And now the night is bleeding
You have topped the needing
And now I have found
I have found the sound of your eyes

Mercy Merges Love

At the depths and the dirt of the sea
And all that breathes below
The whores that walk beneath the waves
Will say there's money in muck
But I say there's more muck in money
And present times agree

There's a trap beneath the odd eye
There's a fall beneath the toothy smile
Bind them both together and blind out the blitz
Then we agree of where we slip

I tell of all my lucky times
My blessing picked and passed
But often or
Not often not
The monster in me muddles
And thinks of what was wanted from me
Prized from my pocket
Stolen from my soul

The beating heart has kept me above ground
Not the silence in my sense
The beating heart has screamed for mercy
And mercy merges love

Mine Wasn't So Good But Yours Was So Bad

Time should never cost a slog
Shared spaced with another should be split
Your nails are looking so bright
But you have never chipped them
Chipped them waiting on me
A modern man must be old fashioned
But a lady becomes a girl
In fashion she swarmed cheaper
But it cost me oh so much
In jewel I broke my back
And it cannot heal alone
Alone is my final failing
Alone my only success
I travelled time to find a woman
I hope the future keeps one for mine

Homage to Hemingway

The world gives us what we want when we
need it most
For those who cannot cope with its creations
And us that cannot be guided by gifts
No help for the shattered heart
No breath for the battered brain
Then the world will offer us the rope
The knife to the wrist
The gun to the gut

The shattered heart that altered its healing
The battered brain is beaten of breath

If you want to keep the gun from the gut
Then take the world with humour
Of all the things foreseen
Try to trust in time

A Wild Mans Dreams

When hope is your final straw to snap
And chaos comes in dribs and drabs
A lap of humility around a track
A trap of resilience wrapped up slack

Folded in broken promises
Feathered in secrets
Flamed in guilt
Grilled on glass

We're getting old

Old we are and bones agree
Winked we did and life ran free
If I could do it over I'd have met you never and met you younger
I'd have dug in the place that you buried your youth
I'd have climbed the cliff of your childhood cries

In opulence
In fortune
In presence
In past

All of these are a wild man’s dreams

Outlaw

Thank you father
Thank you for the wit
The charm
And the chaos

Thank you father
Thank you for the courage
The anguish
And the adventure

Thankyou father
Thank you for the thirst
The looks
And the lessons

Thank you father
Thank you for the speed
The eyes
And the inquisition

Thank you father
Thank you for the ethics
The strength
And the story

Thank you father
Thank you for the guile
The mind
And the morality

Thanks Dad
Thanks Grandad
Thanks for the fun lad

Wanting Worded Ways

Of all of my wanting worded ways
The last of my heart can never display
Everybody I see is sucked in the race
The throw away rags
The riches from space
Pulled from a part that is far away from their grasp
The throw away rags
The riches from space

Alone in pursuit I pave out a law
With rules that reside from loneliness however raw
My virtues aren't vicious my wanting is plain
The mind that meets mine
The kind that treats time
It's a mile from me it's out of my grasp
The mind that meets mine
The kind that treats time

Graceless life

Deterioration

Are you ready for me to disappear
I'm ready for you to be the one
To put my sturdy trust in you
To put my needy burden on you
To break your heart
To disappear

What a pleasure you have been
Like treasure like streams
Like sleeping grass that fluffs your gold
Like bounding wool that holds your head
I'll break your heart
I'm disappearing

But still
Still once
Once we were
And we will love and last forever

Forever golden love that lasts

Raid Their Mind

Wade into the world I'm ready to write
Raid their mind then start to speak
Change them
Bend them
Embroil them
Leave them as they are
Let them sob
Let them sink
Watch them drown

You're here to speak but you are here dumb
Nobody's here to hear
Maybe a failing in me
Maybe time let me down
Perhaps the climate wants me to drown
When it's all said I'll sink
But when I've sunk nothing will be said
Backed by silence

The tepid tapping scrolling screens
A voice is iced and silent scenes
I'm gone and I'm forgotten
But you're bored and you are breathless
You cannot breathe and life turned rotten
I'm gone and I'm forgotten

Town Alive

The world is locked in love
And spared of smog and smoke
I'll show what I see
But first I must be free

Negative Spiritualty

It felt real it felt warm and it felt spiritual
It felt forceful it felt guided and it felt wrong
The bad was the best part
The guilt was the purest condolence

In life I've not felt much
Maybe the loose end of control spiralling away
In life I've felt it all
There's nothing loose that regards breath

It felt rough it felt raw and it felt right
It felt soft it felt sticky and it felt tight
The part where it felt worst
Was the part where I find most of my thoughts

The push to be parallel with emotion
Is the grip that grabs at my mind
The plane that is about to crash
Is the rush that I chase with sincerity

My Soul Picked Its Dove

I love to look at your dimples stretch
I long to make your manner strike
I want as ever to live in your eyes
To cast and spell your heart in cries
Now is when I choose to live
Now is when I lose my past

In early times I was scared of love
Then that feeling raged and left me beaten
At first in my mind when my heart chose you
A great despair took my souls fair freedom
My head and heart began to argue
My head told my heart not to yell for you
My heart was screaming for lust and love
My heart beat my head as my soul picked its
dove

Climbing Floors

Where do we go
What will we see
Tell me your name
Tell me again
Tell me again

All around
Smiling pause

What if the start
Begins at the end
Spell out your shame
Spell it again
Spell it again

All around
Smiling claws

Why does it seem
The sky doesn't cry
Pour out the rain
Pour it again
Pour it again

All around
Climbing spores

Years start to drag
Pulled through a field
Storing the pain
Store it again
Store it again

All around
Climbing floors

My Story

You'll tell a tailored soulless suit
And swill a side of scent
You can cradle chords that don't exist
You can show me where you should

I'll always be a peasant
I'll always be a loner
I'll always be ungraded
I'll always make you laugh

And when you have no other
Or nothing else that speaks
Then for me you'll only need an ear
As me and mine my story is told

Without mercy moving tales on me are told
Never asked for a narrator
Seduction glamour glory rage
Dealt out in the dealer's discretion

New Born

I'm suffocating in self-slaughter
And gasping for a grain of grit
I'm getting it all wrong
I can't catch a break
Screaming against life's tornado
And my breath needs reminding to spring
I feel like my best falls last
And when I try it's not enough
But I'm going too quick at something that is
too new to me
Suppress me in strength
Forgive me of fear
Cradle me courageous
Pray for me

All of above grant me power and glory
And bless me and mine

Gracious for The Elders

I can never agree with whether I chose them or
they chose me
Men beaten by years
Maybe some type of combined effort
Maybe I was on my knees
Maybe they love me
In almost every day I love them more
Men hiccupping hops
The better ones I've always noticed
Are not obligated to join me at ceremonies
They're nothing mutual to me regarding features
They don't share my blood
The better ones I've always winced
Are by my side by choice
They always share my drunken love
They're just as lost as me
Men beaten by years
Men hiccupping hops
Men alone at heart

A single sperm will claim credit and ownership
But a thousand singing figures formed go further

Dusk

The silence that the night brings
Makes me urge to live for a thousand years
The quiet of the dark
Makes me long to be heard in screams
The solitude of the moonlight
Makes me ache to live a lengthy life in deafness

I beg to be heard
Behind a lens where people read
I beg to never be seen
My failing lurks at destroying my mystery
I plea to be immortal
But not for at least a thousand years

Transatlantic Smack

A stack of stones are tied then taxed
A lack of loans I beg to lax
A pack of prawns are prized then spat
The prawns again are dug then spined
To shift the shite from transparent back
With shitey tides transatlantic smack
And smacked again
And belted once
Pinned with ginger
From slanty darks
And straight in crown
And crowned in whores
I'm smacked again
And trashed with wax

Labour

Let there
Let there be water
Let there
Let there be wine

In the wilderness
In the wild wilderness

Let me put my hands
Upon the earth
Let me put my arms
Around the world

Let there
Be white warm water
Let there
Be running red wine

In the wilderness
In the wests wilderness

Let me put my hands
Upon of the earths crown
And let me put me arms
Around the world's womb

Jim

My friend a real character
More than his father
Celebrated for heroism
Celebrated for invincibility
A hero that stops bulls
But my friend wild at heart
Is a real express of energy
Quill him in politeness
Take his heart and show it to him
My friend is scripted by his own name
He felt his fate ten times

A free spirit guided by butchery
If he knew what he could be
If he took his manners and his depth
If he travelled them in threes

I'd love to cradle my young friend
I'd love to show him warmth
I try at times but he is feral
His wildness is his niche
A drink or puff on me my friend
One whilst you are living
For you can be so much

Fast cars are fast deaths
Fast women are fast fantasies
Take a slow one now and then
A painted nail is a tainted girl
A working woman is wealth

A blistering bomb
A story to be told
But don't make it a cheap one him
Make it a long powerful free one Jim

Gracious Dead

I'm here now and I have a story
It's forgotten
But still its occupants
Its occupants times are ticking
They belong to the dead and I'm helpless
They're part selfish
But more part stupid
In sum they're beautiful in completion
The dead will bury the dead
Beautiful they
And they'd never want to know
They've made a thousand mistakes
But in death they said they're sorry
One or two from me

Goodnight

Symbiotic

Plied pulled tugged around
Mine to pull
Mine to tug around
Fragility in form
But a burst of wild energy
A crest in slow push
My tug to touch
My ply in transparency
My pull that pulls
My form that I cannot form
My plasticine that I cannot bend
My love that won't move
My only
My peace
My sound
My never again
My never more
My never since

Black and Yellow

I am the one you never remember
I'm your safety
Your confidant
Your unicorn

I'm the one you sleep in
I'm your bull shit
Your head fart
Your carriage

I'm the quick one
The one you never recognise
Nor thank again
You'll never see me

I'm your midnight rug
I'm your fib like love

I keep your secrets safe by me
Pressed in a pocket of speed and motion
With nothing but fluid to stem it

I'm the one you never remember
I'm your black and yellow

Graciously Wanting to Give

Forever wanting to froth
Permission for something promiscuous
Lustfully wanting to lie
Starving for something savage

I wish to part with myself
A moment in misogyny
I want to exit myself in an act
An act that's shared

Graciously wanting to give
Tempted for something to tease
Painfully wanting to please
Frantic for something frustrating

I wish for relief
A moment in rage
I want to shake then stop
And pause in pleasure

Smog

I can spend the day inebriated
I can pass out in the night
But I pull myself up each morning
My price is sold in swallows
And I wish I'd swallowed more
I cannot live without you
So I won't
I will be treated to first degree humbleness
Twice or thrice a year
Twice or thrice a year
My glory belongs to you
And my glory will always be stationed
A stationary glow
What you mean to me
I couldn't make it rhyme
A politician's pit
He used you as a slut
He told the shiny people
To flourish or to die
He said you were the death of them
If they slipped up in their life

But me I know you better
Your children are so humble
Your children are resourceful
Your children make me laugh
And in your own existence
The place not learned to love
To love my gorgeous town
You never needed teaching
As that implies you're blind
But who would never know
Your beauty in its modesty
Its modest bespoke glow
Tailored to your heart
Those shiny shimmery people
Tell you she's a whore
Well I like to indulge
In its honest dishonesty
Twice or thrice a year
I come to press its pollution
I come to kiss its charisma
I come to fuck its fragility
And I come away discontent
Discontent in my familiarity
As I come away

They personally polluted us
And kept us from our colours
You cut us into quarters
And quarters more and more
You haven't lived in heaven
Where everybody knows your face
They know you have a story
And here and now in people
They want to hear it bleed

Hierophant

This is my dungeon
This is my art house
My sanctuary
I leave my robes at the door
No other door
I like to pop lids and pour
For me the cold will never breach
I shall never feel the cold
The warmth bullies the crevices
It's prolific
Would you like to know what I think of you
Or what you are to me
You are unavoidable
You are inevitable
You are sure
You are fated

Would you like to know what makes me
love you
You with such a young wise head
Would choose mystery and bewilderment
Over cause and reason
You choose
You choose to love things as they are
You don't need a reason
You
I believe that my spirit is screaming
It's screaming to be free
I have no choice
I don't get to choose
But I choose
I choose to give in and be free
I wish not to belong
Not again

Blessed Witch

Steered towards a career in Korea
Never mine
Never mind

Chemistry could have been bought
But a hard sale isn't natural
And theft is against the law
My law

Why would I buy what I sell

A picture should never tell lies
And belief in a fib is denial
But conned I wanted to be
I wanted to be

Why die in a web that I spun

There was something I couldn't evade
It couldn't go unseen
An invention
However unintentional
Cannot be un-invented
Fortunately
Unfortunately
An observation of its own
Obtuse
Obsessive not
Another of many obstacles
Against just one single glorious way

Does glory come at a cost
Or is natures promise
To the good soul
The white heart
The brown skin
And the black heel

Held and healed
Rocked on roses
Of every colour
Calmed in chemicals
Worked not willed

The bask in borrowed blood
To share my favourite sound in unison
To let the lot got hot then cold
I'm yet to see this film
Neither have I written it
And that's what pulls me back
As I'm yet to pick my brains
And I'm yet to pull my veins
And all of this in momentum
Means barely a thing to us both

Sneered by a career in Korea
Never mine
Never mind

Respect never had to be bought
I think of it something unmissable
Missing people is against the law
My law

Why would I buy into absence

Admiration in complete honesty
The truth tells itself as ever
I always wanted to tell you
I always

To die in a web that I spun

Starlit Harmony

Tonight on my journey I looked at the stars
On my course for the first time
I looked at the stars
They love one another
They shine together
Spark together
They don't wish to outdo one another
To be brighter than their neighbours
They shine together
They spark together
And they love one another
For which it begs to be asked
Why in my thirty
Have I never felt the word peace
The idea peace
The concept peace
The warmth of peace
Peace
Why have I never known it breathe
Or felt its breath
Some say that stars are people

Some say they are the most striking things we will see
Can we learn from these dear shimmers
They cannot speak
This is true
But their actions scream to be learned from
They speak through their light
And a lesson in kindness
Can be doubled by beauty
Undoubted beauty
And if one day we accept them
We have never had a choice but to let them burn in our yolks
Then why
Why can we not learn from the simplest rules of harmony
From something we say does not speak
Are we deaf

Death Is Collecting

Death is collecting
As the weeds pollute the earth
It's us that need to fight
Fight to help each other
Fight against the weeds

Death is collecting
The weeds have got the numbers
It's us who have the brains
Brains to help each other
Brains against the weeds

Death is collecting
As flowers we stand out
It's us who possess such beauty
Beauty in each other
Beauty against the rotten

Death is collecting
There's colour in us all
It's us that are unique
Unique in soul and spirit
Unique in our ideas

A cull of beauty is certain
And condemned we are to die
A simpleton belongs to majority
And weeds will never die

We are daises
We are daffodils
We are hunted
We are hung
But we fine-tuned
And we tenacious
We are purposed
We are promised
To live and thrive for just one moment
To adhere and to inspire
To be loved and to love
And of course we get to die

Nobody remembers a weed
And weeds have to live forever
A murderous majority
That never passes in pleasure

Death is collecting

Acknowledgements

With special thanks to everybody that influenced and supported me

Jono Hinley
Ryan Richardson
Sophie Christon
Kimberley Heron
Caroline Sherratt
Faye Mcguiness
Zoe Camp
Elli Marriott
Rebecca Duffy
Darren Howell
Alistair Russell
Craig Mcgill
Craig Morton
Jamie Stokes
Vince Anderson
Dave Coleman

Ferenc Gasci
Garry Robinson
Paul Fletcher
Susannah Millard

All of the staff at the Newberry Centre circa August 2003 till March 2005

The Redfearn Unit in Barnsley during the summer of 2011

The staff at James Cook Unversity Hospital's Central Delivery Suite

My close family Clare Lewis, Jamie Lewis, Stephanie Little and Hannah Lewis

Not forgetting my most sincere and greatest gratitude to my partner, mother of my child, my best friend and my muse Lyndsay Duffy

A Message from Michael Lewis

From as early as I can remember I have wanted to be heard. My most fond memories are of growing up with my siblings. I was the youngest of four great kids and the fun we had and the times we spent will never leave me. Since then it feels like the rarity when we get together we let the clock be the decisive factor of how many laughs we have.

I left school ungraded due to poor health and went to work in France laying roads for travellers. Here I learnt a great work ethic and how to keep up with seasoned drinkers.

Since then I've enjoyed wasting days living in the present however my new born son Lennon Jamie Lewis dictates me to take a far more serious outlook on life.

Life in majority has given me a great one

Available worldwide from Amazon

---

www.mtp.agency

www.facebook.com/mtp.agency

@mtp_agency

Printed in Great Britain
by Amazon

56292048R00141